Instruments and Music

Strings

Daniel Nunn

www.raintreepublishers.co.uk
Visit our website to find out
more information about
Raintree books.

To order:
☎ Phone 0845 6044371
🖨 Fax +44 (0) 1865 312263
💻 Email myorders@raintreepublishers.co.uk

Customers from outside the UK please telephone +44 1865 312262

Raintree is an imprint of Capstone Global Library Limited,
a company incorporated in England and Wales having its
registered office at 7 Pilgrim Street, London, EC4V 6LB
– Registered company number: 6695582

Text © Capstone Global Library Limited 2012
First published in hardback in 2012
The moral rights of the proprietor have been asserted.

Edited by Dan Nunn, Rebecca Rissman, and Sian Smith
Designed by Joanna Hinton-Malivoire
Picture research by Mica Brancic
Production by Victoria Fitzgerald
Originated by Capstone Global Library Ltd
Printed and bound in China by Leo Paper Products Ltd

ISBN 978 1 406 22438 2 (hardback)
15 14 13 12 11
10 9 8 7 6 5 4 3 2 1

British Library Cataloguing in Publication Data
Nunn, Daniel.
  Strings. -- (Instruments and music)
  1. Stringed instruments--Juvenile literature.
  I. Title II. Series
  787.1'9-dc22

Acknowledgements
We would like to thank the following for permission to reproduce
photographs: Alamy p. 13 (© Indiapicture/Phulkit Sharma); ©
Capstone Publishers pp. 21 (Karon Dubke), 22 (Karon Dubke); Corbis
p. 12 (© Todd Gipstein); Getty Images pp. 17 (Redferns/Philip Ryalls),
19 (Digital Vision/Peter Dazeley); iStockphoto p. 7 bottom right
(© DNY59); Photolibrary pp. 4 (© Image Source), 7 bottom centre
(Amanaimages/Amana Productions), 8 (Mauritius /Doug Scott), 11
(Photononstop/Bernard Foubert), 16 (Flirt Collection/Chris Rogers), 20
(Tips Italia/Hermes Images), 23 top (imagebroker.net/Peter Schickert),
23 bottom (Mauritius /Doug Scott); Shutterstock pp. 5 (© Richard
Goldberg), 6 (© Arena Creative), 7 left (© Dmitry Skutin), 7 top centre
(© M E Mulder), 7 top right (© Timmary), 9 (© Joyce Marrero), 10 (©
Patrick Hermans), 14 (© eAlisa), 15 (© VlLevi), 18 (© Barone Firenze).

Cover photograph of a Mariachi Band in San Diego, California,
reproduced with permission of © Getty Images (The Image Bank/Brett
Froomer). Back cover photograph of an electric guitar reproduced
with permission of Shutterstock (© Richard Goldberg).

We would like to thank Jenny Johnson, Nancy Harris, Dee Reid, and
Diana Bentley for their assistance in the preparation of this book.

Every effort has been made to contact copyright holders of
material reproduced in this book. Any omissions will be rectified in
subsequent printings if notice is given to the publisher.

Contents

String instruments

guitar

drum

People play many instruments to make music.

string

A string instrument has strings
stretched across it.

People make a sound by touching the strings.

There are many kinds of string instrument.

Plucking

oud

People use their fingers to play some string instruments. This is called plucking.

8

People use their fingers to play
a ukulele.

People use their fingers to play
a balalaika.

People use their fingers to play
a kora.

Using a bow

bow

People use a bow to play other string instruments.

People use a bow to play a sarinda.

People use a bow to play a cello.

People use a bow to play a violin.

Playing string instruments

Some people play string instruments together.

sitar

Some people play string instruments on their own.

Some people play string instruments for work.

Some people play string instruments just for fun!

Making string instruments

Some string instruments are hard
to make.

Some string instruments are easy
to make.

Play your own string instrument

You can play your own string instruments, too!

Picture glossary

bow a stick with horsehairs stretched across it which is used to play some string instruments

plucking pulling and letting go of strings on a musical instrument to make different sounds

Index

Notes for parents and teachers
Before reading
Find examples of string instruments to share with the children. Some online examples with audio can be found at: http://ngfl.northumberland.gov.uk/music/orchestra/string.htm
Can they name any of the instruments? How do they think the instruments are played? Explain that some string instruments are played with a bow (such as the violin) and some are played by hand (such as the guitar). When they play by hand, people move their hands across the strings or gently pull and let go of strings (plucking). Demonstrate if possible.

After reading
Encourage the children to make their own string instrument. Stretch some elastic bands over an old plastic container. You can then pluck the 'strings'. The tighter the 'strings', the higher the sound!

Extra information
The instruments shown on page 7 are: violin (top right), balalaika (bottom right), sanshin (bottom centre), electric guitar (centre), and harp (left).
String instruments have higher and lower strings. This depends on how tight the strings are stretched and how thin or thick they are. High strings are normally very thin, and low strings very thick.